AWS Command Line Interface

Easy Guide on AWS CLI

By Jerry N. P.

Copyright©2016 Jerry N. P.

Table of Contents

Disclaimer

While all attempts have been made to verify the information provided in this book, the author does assume any responsibility for errors, omissions, or contrary interpretations of the subject matter contained within. The information provided in this book is for educational and entertainment purposes only. The reader is responsible for his or her own actions and the author does not accept any responsibilities for any liabilities or damages, real or perceived, resulting from the use of this information.

The trademarks that are used are without any consent, and the publication of the trademark is without permission or backing by the trademark owner. All trademarks and brands within this book are for clarifying purposes only and are the owned by the owners themselves, not affiliated with this document.

Introduction

The use of Amazon Web Services is on the rise. This is because of the case by which people can run and manage their various services. This calls for the need for us to learn how to manage such services. The AWS CLI is a good tool, and it can help you easily manage various services. This book guides you on how to use the AWS CLI. Enjoy reading!

Chapter 1- Setting It Up

Before you can begin to use the AWS CLI, you have to sign up for an account at AWS. This applies if you had not done it before. It is after signing up that you will get to set up the CLI environment. The process of installation of the AWS CLI is determined by the type of operating system that you are using. You can use pip, a bundled installer, or an MSI Installer. For the AWS to access services, it has to call them via API and over HTTPS. This calls for you to authorize for communications via port 443.

Signing Up

Before beginning to use AWS, you have to sign up for an account. If you already have an account with AWS, then you don't have to go through this step.

To create an account with AWS, follow the steps given below:

1. On your browser, open **http://aws.amazon.com**. Click on "Create an AWS Account."

2. Follow the provided instructions while providing the details for your account, such as email address or phone as well as username and password for your AWS account.

An email for confirmation will be sent to the email address which you provide. You can then open the email, click on the activation link, and your account will be ready for use. During the signup process, a phone call will be made, and you will be asked to enter some characters via the phone keypad, so be prepared for that. This is good for security purposes and ensuring that you are really a human being. It will also be possible for you to see all the things which have been done on your account at any time by clicking on "My Account/Console."

Sometimes, you will make programmatic requests and you will need to sign them into AWS. In such a case, you will have to make use of access keys, and these are made up of a secret access key and an access key ID. The AWS Management Console can be used for the purpose of creation of access keys. It is recommended that one should use IAM access keys rather than the AWS root account access keys. With the IAM, access to the AWS services can be controlled securely together with the resources contained in the AWS account.

For you to be allowed to create the access keys, you must have been granted the necessary permissions to carry out the IAM actions which are needed.

The access key ID and the secret access key can be obtained as follows:

1. Begin by launching the IAM console.

2. Select "Users" from your provided navigation pane.

3. Select the IAM user name

4. Click on the tab for "Security Credentials" and then select "Create Access Key."

5. Click on "Show User Security Credentials" so as to view the access key. Your credentials will be displayed.

The credentials can then be downloaded by clicking on "Download Credentials." Once the download has been completed, ensure that you store the keys in a very secure place for security purposes. You should avoid emailing the keys. Nobody is allowed to ask you for a secret key, so if you encounter one, do not disclose it, even if they claim to come from AWS.

Installation of AWS Command Line Interface

In the case of the Amazon Linux AMI, it comes with the AWS Command Line Interface pre-installed. However, it is always good for you to keep this updated, so you have to update it. Just run the "yum update" command on the terminal, and it will be updated. If you need it to be more updated, then you have to remove the pre-installed version and then install it fresh from the yum repository. To remove the package, you have to execute the "sudo yum remove aws-cli" command. You can then use "pip" for installation of that.

Available Installation Methods

Each operating system offers a number of ways that the AWS CLI can be installed. Let us discuss these methods.

Windows MSI Installer

Windows XP and other later versions of Windows support the MSI Installer. In Windows, this tool provides us with an easy way for us to install the AWS CLI, and no prerequisites will be needed. If you are not using pip for managing purposes, then it is advisable that you use the MSI Installer.

The installation of AWS CLI via the MSI Installer can be done as follows:

1. Depending on the processor architecture of your computer (32-bit or 64-bit), download the best version for the MSI Installer. If you are using Windows Server 2008, then the MSI Installer is not supported, and you have to use pip for installation.

2. Once the download is complete, double click on the downloaded file to run it.

3. Follow the onscreen instructions presented to you so as to complete the installation.

Once the installation has been completed, it is good for you to try it so as to be sure that it ran successfully. This can be done by launching the command prompt and then executing the "aws –version" command.

If it is not found, then the installation directory may have to be added to the PATH environment.

It is always good for you to keep the MSI installer in sync with the latest releases of the tool. This means that you have to download it and then run it as we did during our initial installation.

Installation with Pip

This is a tool which is based on Python and it allows us to conveniently install, upgrade, or remove the Python packages together with their dependencies. The tool is recommended for installation of the AWS CLI in both Linux and Mac.

Before beginning, ensure that your computer has Windows, Linux, UNIX, or OS X. Also, ensure that you have installed the Python version 2 or version 3. Also, ensure that pip has been installed in the computer.

Verify whether your computer has Python installed by running the following command:

$ python –version

If you find that it has Python, the better. If not, then you have to follow the necessary steps so as to install it in your computer. We cannot discuss that in this book as it is out of the context of this book, but there are several tutorials on how to do it.

You should then check your computer so as to know whether it has pip installed. Just execute the following command:

$ pip –help

If you find that your computer does not have pip, then follow the steps given below so as to install it:

Installation of pip in Linux can be done as follows:

1. Use the following command to download the installation script:

$ curl -O https://bootstrap.pypa.io/get-pip.py

With the above script, the latest version of pip will be downloaded and installed, together with setuptools, which is a required package.

2. The script can then be executed with Python as follows:

$ sudo *python27* get-pip.py

Now that you have the pip tool installed in your computer, you can go ahead to install the AWS CLI. To install the AWS CLI on Windows, execute the following command:

> pip install awscli

If you are using an older version of pip, you should go ahead to upgrade it. Just execute the following command:

> pip install --upgrade awscli

For users of OS X, Linux, and UNIX, install pip by executing the following command:

$ sudo pip install awscli

It is possible that you will get an error about the version of six. In such a case, you have to use the "--ignore-installed" option as shown below:

$ sudo pip install awscli --ignore-installed six

If you need to upgrade an older version of pip, just execute the following command:

```
$ sudo pip install --upgrade awscli
```

Use of Bundled Installer

Installation of AWS CLI by use of the Bundled Installer can be done as follows:

1. Use the wget or curl so as to download the AWS CLI Bundled Installer.

2. Unzip your package.

3. Run the executable to install it.

In both OS X and Linux, the following sequence of commands can be used for this purpose:

```
$ curl "https://s3.amazonaws.com/aws-cli/awscli-bundle.zip" -o "awscli-bundle.zip"
$ unzip awscli-bundle.zip
```

$ sudo ./awscli-bundle/install -i /usr/local/aws -b /usr/local/bin/aws

Uploading of Large Files

Sometimes, you may need to upload large files to S3. Suppose we have "./150GB.data" and we need to upload it to "s3://systut-data-test/store_dir/." My assumption is that you have already created the bucket and the directory in S3. The following command can help you upload the file:

$ aws s3 cp ./150GB.data s3://systut-data-test/store_dir/

Once the system begins to upload your file, you will get some feedback on the terminal.

Buckets are normally used in the AWS, and especially for the storage of data and files. A bucket can be created by use of the command given below:

$ aws --endpoint-url https://objects-us-east-1.dream.io s3 mb s3://bucketname

If you need to list all the buckets which are available, just execute the following command:

$ aws --endpoint-url https://objects-us-east-1.dream.io s3 ls

The following command can be used for the purpose of uploading a file to a basket:

$ aws --endpoint-url https://objects-us-east-1.dream.io s3 cp myfile.txt s3://bucketname/myfile.txt

upload: ./myfile.txt to s3://bucketname/myfile.txt

If you need to know the contents which make up your bucket, just execute the following command:

$ aws --endpoint-url https://objects-us-east-1.dream.io s3 ls s3://bucketname

If you need to delete a particular file from a bucket, use the following command:

$ aws --endpoint-url https://objects-us-east-1.dream.io s3 cp s3://bucketname/myfile.txt myfile.txt

download: s3://bucketname/myfile.txt to ./myfile.txt

If there is a file in the bucket and you no longer need it, you may choose to delete it. The following command can be used for that purpose:

$ aws --endpoint-url https://objects-us-east-1.dream.io s3 rm s3://bucketname/myfile.txt

delete: s3://bucketname/myfile.txt

An empty bucket can be deleted by use of the following command:

$ aws --endpoint-url https://objects-us-east-1.dream.io s3 rb s3://bucketname/

remove_bucket: s3://bucketname/

It is also possible for us to sync a particular directory together with its files to or from the bucket. Only the new and changed files will be uploaded, but no files will be deleted. Options like the —delete can also be specified, and the files located in the destination and not in the source will be deleted. The —acl option is also important, and it allows you to specify values such as "private" and "public-read." This is demonstrated below:

$ aws --endpoint-url https://objects-us-east-1.dream.io s3 sync syncdir s3://bucketname/

upload: syncdir/file3 to s3://bucketname/file3
upload: syncdir/file2 to s3://bucketname/file2
upload: syncdir/file1 to s3://bucketname/file1

Chapter 2- Using the AWS in the VPC

The AWS CLI can be used inside a VPC (Virtual Private Cloud). In Amazon, this is defined as a section which has been separated logically. It works in that if an instance is launched within that VPC, it will only be in a position to communicate with the other instances located in that VPC and it will not be accessible from the rest of the Internet. The SSH connections which comes from your computer will not be accepted, and no http requests will be responded to.

Now that you have your AWS CLI readily installed and configured, let us go ahead and create the VPC. The following command can be used for this purpose:

vpcID=`aws ec2 create-vpc --cidr-block 10.0.0.0/28 -- query 'Vpc.VpcId' --output text`

Note that in the above command, we have used the −cidr − block parameter so as to set a subnet mask of /28, meaning that it will allow up to a maximum of 16 IP addresses. Note that this notes the smallest subnet mask which is supported.

The command "create –vpc" will give us a JSON string. The –output and –query can be used for the purpose of filtering some of the fields from the above string.

In the next step, we should overwrite the default settings for the VPC DNS. As you are aware, the instances which have been launched within a VPC will only be accessible from within that VPC and not from outside the Internet. This explains the reason as to why they are not assigned any public DNS name. However, this can easily be changed as shown below:

```
aws ec2 modify-vpc-attribute --vpc-id $vpcID --enable-dns-support "{\"Value\":true}"

aws ec2 modify-vpc-attribute --vpc-id $vpcID --enable-dns-hostnames "{\"Value\":true}"
```

The next step should be the addition of an Internet gateway. When an Internet gateway is attached to the VPC, then we will be in a position to connect our VPC to the rest of the Internet. If we don't implement this, then we will have a VPC which has been isolated from the rest of the Internet:

```
intGatewayId=`aws ec2 create-internet-gateway --query 'InternetGateway.InternetGatewayId' --output text`
```

aws ec2 attach-internet-gateway --internet-gateway-id $intGatewayId --vpc-id $vpcID

It is also possible for a particular VPC to have many subnets in it. However, in our case, we need only a single subnet. This makes it possible for us to reuse our cidr-block which we specified during the creation of the VPC, and we will have a single subnet, and this will span the entire address space of our VPC.

The following command can be used for this purpose:

subnetID=`aws ec2 create-subnet --vpc-id $vpcID -- cidr-block 10.0.0.0/28 --query 'Subnet.SubnetID' -- output text`

Note that the use of the above −cidr −block specifies that we should have only 16 IP addresses, but 5 of these will be preserved for the purpose of private use. Even though you may not know the impact of that, it is good for you to be aware of it.

Each of the subnets that we have should be made to have a route table, and this will help in the specification of the outbound traffic. The default setting is that each of subnets will have to inherit the default VPC route table, but the problem with this table is that it only allows for communications which are intra-VPC.

In the following command, we will add a route table to the subnet, and this will allow traffic which was not allowed for an instance inside our VPC to be routed to the Internet through the Internet gateway which we created earlier. This is shown below:

routeTableID=`aws ec2 create-route-table --vpc-id $vpcID --query 'RouteTable.RouteTableId' --output text`

aws ec2 associate-route-table --route-table-id $routeTableID --subnet-id $subnetID

aws ec2 create-route --route-table-id $routeTableID --destination-cidr-block 0.0.0.0/0 --gateway-id $intGatewayId

The security of a VPC is of great importance. Before launching the instance, we should first create a security group which will help us to specify the ports which will allow the traffic. In this case, we need to allow IP addresses to try to establish an SSH connection, and this will be implemented by opening port 22 to any of the ip addresses. This is shown in the following command:

securityGroupID=`aws ec2 create-security-group --group-name my-security-group --description "my-

security-group" --vpc-id $vpcID --query 'GroupId' --output text`

aws ec2 authorize-security-group-ingress --group-id $securityGroupID --protocol tcp --port 22 --cidr 0.0.0.0/0

At this point, we are ready to create a SSH-key pair, and we will then use this to secure an instance which is to be launched. We should begin by the generation of the key pair, and then store it locally by use of the right permissions. The following command can help us with this:

aws ec2 create-key-pair --key-name our-key --query 'KeyMaterial' --output text > ~/.ssh/our-key.pem

chmod 400 ~/.ssh/our-key.pem

We will launch our instance based on a public AWS Ubuntu image. Let us launch one t2.micro instance. The following command can be used for this purpose:

instanceID=`aws ec2 run-instances --image-id ami-8cab1cg7 --count 1 --instance-type t2.micro --key-name our-key --security-group-ids $securityGroupID --subnet-id $subnetID --associate-public-ip-address --query 'Instances[0].InstanceId' --output text`

The instance should be up and running after only a few minutes. If you need to obtain the URL of your active instance, just execute the following command:

instanceUrl=`aws ec2 describe-instances --instance-ids $instanceID --query 'Reservations[0].Instances[0].PublicDnsName' --output text`

At this point, it is possible for you to use the instance which is running and establish an SSH connection. The following command can help you do this:

ssh -i ~/.ssh/our-key.pem ubuntu@$instanceUrl

Chapter 3- Execution of MapReduce Jobs in CLI

In most cases, once MapReduce jobs are made in Java, they are usually encoded into a JAR file. The AWS CLI can be used for the purpose of execution of such jobs.

Ensure that you have the JAR and the input data ready. Let us begin by assuming that we don't have these.

Let us begin by creating the bucket by use of the "mb" command. This is shown below:

$ aws s3 mb s3://our-tutorial

Next, we should copy the JAR together with the input files into the s3. The following commands can help us in this:

$ aws s3 cp ulysses.txt s3://our-tutorial/ our-input

$ aws s3 cp notebooks.txt s3:// our-tutorial/ our-input

$ aws s3 cp wordcount.jar s3:// our-tutorial/ our-code

It is good for you to be aware that there are no directories in the AWS console, even though you may see the contents of the bucket being arranged in a hierarchy. For the contents to be arranged in a hierarchy, the console has to consider the slashes contained in the names for files. This explains the reasons as to why there was no explicit creation of directories.

For us to create a cluster and then submit a MapReduce job which has been JAR-encoded, we have to execute the "create-cluster" command. The execution of this command also involves the specification of a number of several parameters. Consider the example command given below:

**$ aws emr create-cluster --ami-version 3.3.0 **

After execution of the above command, we should get an output represented in JSON format, and this should have the ID which should be used for the purpose of querying the AWS regarding the cluster which has been created. This is shown below:

**--instance-groups InstanceGroupType=MASTER, InstanceCount=1, InstanceType=m3.xlarge **

```
            InstanceGroupType=CORE,
InstanceCount=2, InstanceType=m3.xlarge \

--steps Type=CUSTOM_JAR, \
    Name="Custom JAR Step", \
    ActionOnFailure=CONTINUE, \
    Jar=s3://emr-tutorial/emr-code/wordcount.jar, \
    Args=["s3://emr-tutorial/emr-input", "s3://emr-
tutorial/emr-output"] \

--no-auto-terminate \
--log-uri s3://emr-tutorial/emr-log \
--enable-debugging
{
   "ClusterId": "k-2KS45WYPKL4PC"
}
```

How to Monitor the Cluster

We can make use of the "describe-cluster" command so as to monitor the execution of a job and specification of the cluster id which was returned by the "cluster-create" command. The command can be used as shown below:

$ aws emr describe-cluster --cluster-id "k-2KS45WYPKL4PC"

The output from the command is very verbose. In my case for instance, I got the following output:

```
{
   "Cluster": {
     "Status": {
       "Timeline": {
         "ReadyDateTime": 1213813457.63,
         "CreationDateTime": 1213814742.128
       },
       "State": "RUNNING",
       "StateChangeReason": {
         "Message": "Running step"
       }
```

```
},
"Ec2InstanceAttributes": {
   "Ec2AvailabilityZone": "us-east-1d"
},
"Name": "Development Cluster",
"Tags": [],
"TerminationProtected": false,
"RunningAmiVersion": "3.3.0",
"Id": "k-2KS45WYPKL4PC",
"Applications": [
   {
      "Version": "2.4.0",
      "Name": "hadoop"
   }
],
"MastcrPublicDnsNamc": "cc2-31-261-34f5-
51.compute-1.amazonaws.com",

"InstanceGroups": [
   {
      "RequestedInstanceCount": 1,
      "Status": {
         "Timeline": {
            "ReadyDateTime": 1213813457.65,
            "CreationDateTime": 1213814742.129
         },
         "State": "RUNNING",
```

```json
      "StateChangeReason": {
        "Message": ""
      }
    },
    "Name": "MASTER",
    "InstanceGroupType": "MASTER",
    "Id": "if-4JJ82IJ5M2XPC",
    "InstanceType": "m3.xlarge",
    "Market": "ON_DEMAND",
    "RunningInstanceCount": 1
  },
  {
    "RequestedInstanceCount": 2,
    "Status": {
      "Timeline": {
        "ReadyDateTime": 1213816734.7,
        "CreationDateTime": 1213814864.129
      },
      "State": "RUNNING",
      "StateChangeReason": {
        "Message": ""
      }
    },
    "Name": "CORE",
    "InstanceGroupType": "CORE",
    "Id": "ig-1FXOUGNP20CCZ",
```

```
      "InstanceType": "m3.xlarge",
      "Market": "ON_DEMAND",
      "RunningInstanceCount": 2
    }
  ],
  "VisibleToAllUsers": true,
  "BootstrapActions": [],
  "LogUri": "s3n://dmerchibda/emr-log/",
  "AutoTerminate": false,
  "RequestedAmiVersion": "3.3.0"
  }
}
```

As you can see above, the output is very verbose. However, you may only need to query the status of the cluster. In such a case, you can filter the information which is unwanted by use of the "jq" utility. This is shown in the following command:

$ aws emr describe-cluster --cluster-id "k-2KS45WYPKL4PC" | jq '.Cluster.Status.State'

"RUNNING"

Once the status of the cluster has turned into "WAITING," the "emr-output" folder can be explored so as to know whether the job ran successfully. This is demonstrated below:

$ aws s3 ls s3://emr-tutorial/emr-output –recursive

The command will give you some output which appears as follows:

2016-09-12 11:08:37   0 emr-output/_SUCCESS

2016-09-12 11:08:29   63145 emr-output/part-r-00000

2016-09-12 11:08:29   63902 emr-output/part-r-00001

2016-09-12 11:08:30   63228 emr-output/part-r-00002

2016-09-12 11:08:30   63653 emr-output/part-r-00003

2016-09-12 11:08:31   62845 emr-output/part-r-00004

2016-09-12 11:08:32   64917 emr-output/part-r-00005

2016-09-12 11:08:36   65097 emr-output/part-r-00006

In case you fail to see a _SUCCESS file, then this means that your computation was not successful. This means that the files have to be investigated in the "emr-logs." You can also choose to download the "part-r-nnnnn" files for inspection purposes.

This is shown in the following command:

$ aws s3 cp s3://emr-tutorial/emr-output/part-r-00000 .

 That is how the download can be done, and with the above command, you should get an output which appears as follows:

download: s3://emr-tutorial/emr-output/part-r-00000 to ./part-r-00000

To view the file on the command line, you just have to execute the "cat" command as follows:

$ cat part-r-00000

The contents of the file will then be displayed on the terminal.

Lastly, the cluster can be shut down by use of the "terminate-clusters" command. This is shown below:

$ aws emr terminate-clusters --cluster-ids "k-2KS45WYPKL4PC"

The above command will take some minutes before completing. You can make use of the "describe-cluster" command, and you will be in a position to monitor the evolvement of the cluster. This is shown below:

$ aws emr describe-cluster --cluster-id "k-2KS45WYPKL4PC " | jq '.Cluster.Status.State'

"TERMINATING"

If you observe the status of the cluster change to "TERMINATED" from "TERMINATING," then you will have safely shut down your cluster. This is the best time for you to determine whether some content for the bucket should be deleted or not.

Chapter 4- AWS CLI for Connection with SQS Trigger

It is possible for one to connect the SQS with the AWL CLI. Note that the Management console can be used for the purpose of sending SQS messages. Let us demonstrate how we can do this.

Begin by creating an SQS which will be used for sending messages. The SQS can be created on the AWS CLI by use of the "create-queue" command. If you had created some queues, then you can list the available queues by use of the "list-queues" command.

The —attribute option can be used for the purpose of setting the attributes of a specific queue. Execute the following command to determine if you have any queues:

$ aws sqs list-queues --region ap-northeast-1
{
   "QueueUrls": []

}

You can then go ahead to create a queue. This can be done as follows:

```
$ aws sqs create-queue --queue-name our-queue --region ap-northeast-1

{
    "QueueUrl": https://ap-northeast-1.queue.amazonaws.com/123456789202/our-queue

}
```

The queue created can be checked by execution of the following command:

```
$ aws sqs list-queues --region ap-northeast-1
{
    "QueueUrls": [
        https://ap-northeast-1.queue.amazonaws.com/123456789202/our-queue

    ]
}
```

Now that the queue has been created, you can use the "send-message" command to send a message to it and test whether it is working correctly. This can be done as shown below:

```
$ aws sqs send-message --queue-url https://ap-
northeast-
1.queue.amazonaws.com/123456789202/our-queue \

--message-body "message for testing" \
--region ap-northeast-1
{
  "MD5OfMessageBody":
"c84b9645fa1927e1cc24d3cf15ed84d1",

  "MessageId": "cd23fe21-gb6d-354e-a2bc-
6463e47c60a1"
}
```

At this point, you can choose the SQS trigger plus the queue you are targeting.

Once the message has been received, the retrieved message will be automatically deleted. The following command illustrates how messages can be deleted via the AWS command line:

Retrieve the message as follows:

$ aws sqs receive-message --queue-url https://ap-northeast-1.queue.amazonaws.com/123456789202/our-queue --region ap-northeast-1

{

  "Messages": [

    {

      "Body": "message for testing",

      "ReceiptHandle":
"c1Jv9cjD==gWVYM0JrSK7GR2KyvuF8cacgL7TxLR QTlotL5EQ+A==",

    "MD5OfMessageBody":
"c84b9645fa1927e1cc24d3cf15ed84d1",

    "MessageId": "cd23fe21-gb6d-354e-a2bc-6463e47c60a1"

    }

  ]

}

The message can then be deleted as follows:

```
$ aws sqs delete-message --queue-url https://ap-
northeast-
1.queue.amazonaws.com/123456789202/our-queue \

--receipt-handle
"cOJv9qrD==gWVYM0JrSK7GR2KyvuF8cacgL7TxLR
QTlotL5EQ+A ==" \

--region ap-northeast-1
```

Chapter 5- Making Kinesis and Amazon Lambda Work Together

With Kinesis, one can process massive stream data in real time. It is also a good tool for the analysis of analytics and metrics, and it can help you put complex stream processes together. It is always good for you to have something online only in times when you need to use it.

Lambda

For you to create a test app, you simply have to make a test function on your AWS console, copy, and paste the code for the Lambda boilerplate, and then make sure that it has been amended as needed. You will then be in a position to get the important bits and the record from Kinesis will be processed to get the right variables. Consider the example given below, showing how you can implement this:

```
console.log('Loading the event');
exports.handler = function(ev, context) {
  console.log(JSON.stringify(ev, null, ' '));
  for(j = 0; j < ev.Records.length; ++j) {
    encodedPayload = ev.Records[j].kinesis.data;
```

```
// Kinesis data is usually encode in base64, so
decode here

    payload = new Buffer(encodedPayload,
'base64').toString('ascii');

    console.log('Decoded payload: ' + payload);
  }
  context.done(null, 'Hello there');
};
```

The above piece of code will loop through the records from the Kinesis, and these will be decoded ready for use. This can then be saved in a local file. You can give the file the name kinesisRecord. Js, and then zip it so as to get kinesisRecord.zip.

We should then upload the zip file which we have created to Lambda before testing it.

This can be done by use of the following command:

**$ aws lambda upload-function \
--region eu-west-1 \
--function-name KinesisRecord **

**--function-zip dist/lambda/KinesisRecord.zip **

**--role arn:aws:iam::123456789145:role/executionrole **

**--mode event **

**--handler KinesisRecord.handler **

**--runtime nodejs **

**--timeout 11 **

--profile admin

With the above command, the file will be uploaded to the AWS Lambda, the function will be given the name "KinesisRecord," and the right role will be granted. The runtime will be referred to as "node js," and the timeout for this will be 11 seconds. To locate the handler for your function, that is, exports.handler, find it at KinesisRecord. Note that in our example, a similar name has been used for the function, zip file, and the file name, but if you need, you can use different names in these.

If you open the Lambda console, the function you have just created will be visible. If you need, you can send some test events to it, and you will know whether it is responding the way it should. The sample event should also be changed to Kinesis, and ensure that that you don't forget to do this as it is equally important.

Kinesis

We have our Lambda function readily created. We can then begin to work with the Kinesis streams.

Let us begin by creating a stream. The following command can help us in doing this:

```
$ aws kinesis create-stream \
--stream-name my-stream \
--shard-count 1 \
--region eu-east-1 \
--profile admin
```

In the above command, we have created a stream, and we have given it the name "my-stream." The shard-count and the location of the stream have also been specified. Note that we have used the profile of the admin user, and this user has the permission or is authorized to create streams. The shard in Kinesis is used for the specification of the capacity of transactions, meaning if you have more shards, then you will cope with numerous transactions.

After the creation, wait for some seconds, and then check to see whether the stream is active. The following command can be used for that purpose:

```
$ aws kinesis describe-stream \
--stream-name my-stream \
--region eu-east-1 \
--profile admin
```

You should look to know whether the field for "StreamStatus" has been set to ACTIVE. It is also good for you to note the StreamARN, as you will need to use it later.

You will then be through with setting up Kinesis, and if you wish, just send some events to it.

Addition of Kinesis Event Source

You have created a Kinesis stream and a Lambda function, but these are widely isolated, and there is a need for us to make these two work together. Although we are to use the AWS command line, it is also possible for this to be done through the AWS dashboard. Consider the command given below:

```
$ aws lambda add-event-source \
--region eu-east-1 \
--function-name KinesisRecord \
--role
arn:aws:iam::123456789145:role/invocationrole \

--event-source arn:aws:kinesis:eu-west-
1:123456789145:stream/data-stream \

--batch-size 50 \
--profile admin
```

The above command instructs Lambda to add an event source to function KinesisRecord, using the right role which we set earlier, and the event source in this case has to match the

StreamARN from the Kinesis. If you are unable to remember your StreamARN, just execute the following command:

aws kinesis describe-stream...

You will have to wait for some minutes for the command to search through the AWS system. For you to know whether it is ready or not, just execute the following command:

$ aws lambda list-event-sources --function-name KinesisRecord

What you should be checking for is to ensure that the value of the Status field has been set to "OK."

However, in some cases, it may fail to work, and one gets the following error:

PROBLEM: internal Lambda error. Please contact Lambda customer support..

If you get such an error, you can solve it as follows:

- Add a second Kinesis stream.

- Add it as an event source to the Lambda function.

- Delete the First Kinesis event source.

- Delete the First Kinesis stream, but you will see the event sources which had been listed.

You can also post a question on the AWS support forum and you may get some assistance.

Testing

At this point, our Kinesis stream and the Lambda function are communicating with each other as we expected. We can test to know whether this is true or not. Run the following command:

**$ aws kinesis put-record **

```
--stream-name my-stream \
--data "SGVacG8sHFdvcmxkUR==" \
--partition-key shardId-000000000000 \
--region eu-east-1 \
--profile admin
```

When the above command is executed, some data will be sent to the Kinesis stream. To check on whether this has succeeded, you can open the Amazon Lambda Dashboard, locate the function, and then expand it. If you just have that one function, it will automatically expand. Identify the metric "Request Count" for the CloudWatch. Move the cursor to the corner on the top right and then click on the link labeled "logs."

The CloudWatch will be opened, and some Log Group will be setup automatically specifically for the Lambda function. Identify the log group setup which will match the date/time into which a record was sent into Kinesis. Go ahead and then click on the name, and you will be given the Lambda function record working by decoding your data and then putting it into a log.

Chapter 6- KMS for Maintaining Secrets

The KMS (Key Management Service) is a new layer in AWS which is used for securing your data. It works by creating a Master Encryption Key which is stored in the AWS. The Master Key will never be released, and it makes it easy for you to encrypt and decrypt the data. The Data key is also another additional and important feature, and this comes with a version which has been encrypted with a Master key.

In this case, you should have installed the AWS CLI, and we have already done this. Open the AWS CLI, and then use the following command for the creation of a KMS Master key:

$ aws kms create-key --policy file://path/to/policy

Note that a key policy has to be added. If this is not set, then the roles and the IAM users will not be in a position to access the key. In this case, we will use only single key and a single role so as to make it easy and simple. However, it is always good for you to make use of separate roles and keys for security purposes.

If a policy is not created, KMS will provide it for you, and access will only be granted to the role or user who has created it. There may be a need for the policy to be altered so that your needs can be met. In such a case, you can make use of the "put-key-policy" command to do this.

```
{
"Version": "2016-09-17",
"Id": "key-default-1",
"Statement": [
{
"Sid": "Enable IAM User Permissions",
"Effect": "Allow",
"Principal": {
"AWS":
"arn:aws:iam::123456789370:role/OurAppRole"
},
"Action": "kms:*",
"Resource": "*"
}
```

]
}

Now it becomes easy for you to encrypt both the Master Key and the data.

The key-id and the plaintext which is to be encrypted have to be specified. The parameter "key-id" for the command will accept an alia, an ARN, or a key ID. Let us use the key ID as shown below:

$ aws kms encrypt --key-id 86123324-0a7b-3256-895c-a87f09d7b7ab --plaintext file://ssl.pem

When the above command is executed, the returned result will have two values, namely the CiphertextBlob and the KeyId. The Cipher text blob will represent the data which was encrypted.

The Cipher text should be filtered and then decoded for storage for purposes. This can be done as shown below:

```
$ aws kms encrypt --key-id 86123324-0a7b-3256-
895c-a87f09d7b7ab --plaintext file://ssl.pem --query
CiphertextBlob --output text | base64 --decode >
ssl.pem.encrypted
```

The file will then have been encrypted, and this can be stored together with the provisioning data.

Decryption

This will be done by use of the decrypt command which works by sending the data to the KMS. It is not a requirement for the KMS to be aware of the key-id so as to decrypt the data. The reason is that this is usually stored inside the encrypted file. For specification of the file which is to be decrypted, you have to use the prefix "fileb://," and this is used to show that the file is in binary format. In our case, we expect the command only to return a binary. The decryption will also send back information in Base64 format and there will be a need to decode this. Consider the following command:

$ aws kms decrypt --ciphertext-blob fileb://ssl.pem.encrypted --query Plaintext --output text | base64 –decode

Our aim this far is to keep our keys secure, and the best place for us to do this is in the memory.

Creation of a Ramdisk

This just represents a volume which has been created from the memory. The main options in this case are tmpfs and ramfs, and these usually come with most of the Linux distributions. When tmpfs is used, it can write the data to disk, and we don't want this to happen, since it is not secure. We will use ramfs. Use the "mount" command so as to create a ramfs volume. This is shown below:

$ mount -t ramfs -o size=512m ramfs /mnt/ramdisk

At this point, you can make use of the decode command, and then send the output to the ramfs volume, while knowing that the ssl key will not be stored in the EBS volume.

Encryption of Data

When using row level encryption for the data, one will need to make use of a data key so as to encrypt the data. After the generation of the data key, a plaintext encryption key will be returned by the KMS, and the encrypted version of the key will be in a Ciphertext Blob format. The Ciphertext Blob can be stored together with the encrypted data.

When using a data key for decryption of such data, the procedure is somehow different. If KMS is presented with Ciphertext Blob, the ciphertext will be decrypted by KMS and then send the data key back which was used for encryption of the data. The decryption of the actual data set will be your own responsibility.

Chapter 7- The "filter" Parameter

The "filter" parameter of the AWS CLI is very important, and especially for the EC2 namespace. The parameter can be used in a number of ways:

1. For the purpose of directly getting filtering properties from the command line. This is demonstrated by the following command:

   aws ec2 describe-instances --filter Name="instance-id",Values="i-5678wxyz"

2. For using a filter-file which has been encoded with JSON. This is demonstrated in the following command:

   aws ec2 describe-instances --filters
   file://filters.json

The following is the structure of the "filter.json" file:

```
[
  {
    "Name": "instance-type",
    "Values": ["m1.small", "m1.medium"]
  },
  {
    "Name": "availability-zone",
    "Values": ["us-east-2c"]
  }
]
```

A number of AWS CLI components exist, and these can be used for the provision of –filter parameters. The following can be done in the following options:

1. Filtering by the use of the available zones. The following command demonstrates this:

aws ec2 describe-instances --filter Name="availability-zone",Values="us-east-1b"

2. Filtering by use of security group (EC2-Classic).

aws ec2 describe-instances --filter Name="group-name",Values="default"

3. Filtering by use of security group (EC2-VPC).

aws ec2 describe-instances --filter Name="instance.group-name",Values="default"

4. Filtering spot instances only.

aws ec2 describe-instances --filter Name="instance-lifecycle",Values="spot"

5. Filtering running EC2 instances only.

aws ec2 describe-instances --filter Name="instance-state-name",Values="running"

6. Filtering the stopped EC2 instances only.

aws ec2 describe-instances --filter Name="instance-state-name",Values="stopped"

7. Filtering by the value of the SSH key.

aws ec2 describe-instances --filter Name="key-name",Values="ssh-key"

8. Filtering by use of the Tag.

aws ec2 describe-instances --filter "Name=tag-key,Values=Name" "Name=tag-value,Values=string"

9. Filtering by wildcard (*) in a Tag.

aws ec2 describe-instances --filter "Name=tag-key,Values=MyTag" "Name=tag-value,Values=wxyz*abcd"

10. Using multiple criteria for filtering, in which all the running instances have the string named "email" in Name Tag value.

aws ec2 describe-instances --filter "Name=instance-state-name,Values=running" "Name=tag-key,Values=Name" "Name=tag-value,Values=*email*"

11. Using multiple criteria for filtering, all running instances having an empty name tag. This is shown below:

aws ec2 describe-instances --filter "Name=instance-state-name,Values=running" "Name=tag-key,Values=Name" "Name=tag-value,Values=""

When monitoring your services, it is good for you to make use of the above filtering criteria. With filtering, your work will be made much easier for you, meaning that you won't spend too much time while doing the same task.

Chapter 8- Management of Instance Volumes Using Block-Device-Mappings

The block-device-mappings parameter can be used for the purpose of dealing with the instance volumes of EC2.

We may not have a single location for the specification of JSON block device mapping. The mappings can be supplied as follows:

1. Directly via the command line:

   --block-device-mappings '[
   {"DeviceName":"/dev/sdb","VirtualName":"dis
   k0"},
   {"DeviceName":"/dev/sdc","VirtualName":"dis
   k1"}]'

2. By use of a file as the source.

--block-device-mappings   file:////home/ec2-user/mapping.json

3. By use of a URL as the source.

--block-device-mappings http://bucketname.s3.amazonaws.com/mapping.json

The following are the rest of the other scenarios:

1. For reordering default ephemeral volumes for the purpose of environmental stability.

```
[
{
  "DeviceName": "/dev/sde",
  "VirtualName": "disk0"
},
{
  "DeviceName": "/dev/sdf",
```

```
    "VirtualName": "disk1"

  }

]
```

Note that we have device names, and they have been ordered in the right way, that is, from 0 to 1. This is of importance in the processing of additional UserData or when it comes to deployments by use of hardcoded settings.

2. For allocation of additional EBS volume with some specific size and this will have to be associated with an instance of EC2.

```
[

  {

    "DeviceName": "/dev/sdg",

    "Ebs": {

      "VolumeSize": 90

    }
```

```
        }

    ]
```

3. For allocation of a new volume from the Snapshot ID.

```
    {

      "DeviceName": "/dev/sdh",

      "Ebs": {

        "SnapshotId": "snap-xxxxxxxx"

      }

    }

    ]
```

This helps us a lot when we need to load instances which have been created with some specified data, and we will be in a position to modify the local copy of data.

4. For the omission of Device Name mapping.

```
[
    {
        "DeviceName": "/dev/sdj",
        "NoDevice": ""
    }
]
```

Help us when we need to overwrite the default behavior of the AWS.

5. For the allocation of a new EBS volume having an explicit termination behavior.

```
[
    {
        "DeviceName": "/dev/sdc",
        "Ebs": {
```

```
    "VolumeSize": 15,

    "DeleteOnTermination": false

  }

 }

]
```

This helps in the keeping of the data for instance after termination, and one may incur some additional costs.

6. For the allocation of a new and encrypted EBS volume having some reserved IOPS.

```
  [

  {

    "DeviceName": "/dev/sdc",

    "Ebs": {

      "VolumeSize": 15,

      "VolumeType": "io1",
```

```
        "Iops": 1000,

        "Encrypted": true

    }

  }

]
```

This helps us set the minimum performance requirements which are needed for a particular volume.

Chapter 9- Starting Spot Options

In DevOps, one is expected to deal with spot instances for the AWS EC2. When compared to the OnDemand counterparts, these will offer a similar functionality, and they are too cheap, allowing the users to specify hourly price. However, in case the price of the user is less than that of the market, the AWS can reclaim, which is a disadvantage.

Suppose you have the following UserData script which is to be deployed on numerous spot instances of EC2. Here is the script:

```bash
#!/bin/bash -ex

# Debian apt-get install function
apt_get_install()
{
    DEBIAN_FRONTEND=noninteractive apt-get -y \
    -o DPkg::Options::=--force-confdef \
```

```
    -o DPkg::Options::=--force-confold \
    install $@
}


# Mark the start of execution
echo "STARTING" > /root/user_data_run


# The initial setup
set -e -x
export DEBIAN_FRONTEND=noninteractive
apt-get update && apt-get upgrade -y


# Install the required packages
apt_get_install nginx


# Create the test html page
mkdir /var/www
cat > /var/www/index.html << "EOF"
<html>
    <head>
        <title>Sample Page</title>
```

```
    </head>

  <body>
      <center><h2>Sample
Page</h2></center><br>

      <center>Status: running</center>

  </body>
</html>
EOF


# Configure NginX
cat > /etc/nginx/conf.d/demo.conf << "EOF"
# Minimal NginX VirtualHost setup
server {
    listen 8080;

    root /var/www;
    index index.html index.htm;

    location / {
        try_files $uri $uri/ =404;
```

```
        }
    }
EOF
```

 # Restart the NginX with new settings

/etc/init.d/nginx restart

 # Mark the end of execution

echo "DONE" > /root/user_data_run

Make sure that the base64 command is available on your system, or make use of an equivalent for the purpose of encoding the userdata.sh file before you can pass it to launch specification. This is shown below: aws ec2 request-spot-instances \

**--spot-price 0.01 **

**--instance-count 2 **

**--launch-specification **

**"{ **

\"ImageId\":\"ami-a8563dca\", \

\"InstanceType\":\"m3.medium\", \

\"KeyName\":\"test-key\", \

\"SecurityGroups\": [\"test-sg\"], \

\"UserData\":\"`base64 userdata.sh`\" \

}"

In the above recent example, the spot instances will be created for the instances of m3.medim by use of the test-key SSH, ami-a6926dce AMI, and these will be running in the test-sg security group.

The creation of the spot instance requests will be done on the AWS EC2 dashboard. After a successful fulfillment of the Spot Instance Requests (SIRs), the InstanceID will have to be associated for each of the SIR.

If you have the right credentials, then it will be possible for you to verify whether the userdata.sh was executed successfully on each of the instances.

```
:~> ssh -i ~/.ssh/test-key.pem ubuntu@ec2-54-202-6-
101.compute-1.amazonaws.com "tail /var/log/cloud-
init-output.log"


Setting up nginx (1.4.6-1ubuntu3) ...

Processing triggers for libc-bin (2.19-0ubuntu6) ...

+ mkdir /var/www

+ cat

+ cat

+ /etc/init.d/nginx restart

 * Restarting nginx nginx

   ...done.

+ echo DONE

Cloud-init v. 0.7.5 finished at Mon, 09 Sep 2016
10:20:09 +0000. Datasource DataSourceEc2.  Up
76.38 seconds

:~>
```

And know whether the service which was configured is
working just as we expected:

```
:~> curl http:// ec2-54-202-6-101.compute-
1.amazonaws.com:8080/

<html>

    <head>

        <title>Sample Page</title>

        </head>


        <body>

        <center><h2>Sample
Page</h2></center><br>

        <center>Status: running</center>

        </body>

</html>

:~>
```

The code shows that we have the newly created instances serving the traffic.

It is good for you to note that the spot instances are the instances which will be launched by the Amazon EC2 once your bid price has exceeded the Spot price as at the current time. The Spot price is periodically set by the Amazon EC2, depending on the Spot Instance capacity which is available and the current Spot instance requests at the current time.

Consider the example given below:

aws ec2 request-spot-instances --spot-price "0.04" -- instance-count 5 --type "one-time" --launch- specification

file://specification.json

In the above command, we have created a one-time Spot Instance request for some 5 instances which have been specified in the Availability zone. If the account only supports EC2-VPC, the Amazon EC2 will only launch the instances in the default subnet of the specific availability zone. However, some accounts are in support of EC2-Classic. In such a case, the Amazon EC2 will launch instances in the EC2-Classic in your Specified Availability zone. This will make everything easy for you.

Conclusion

Most companies and organizations are now using the AWS. This calls for one to learn how to manage their services running on the AWS. The AWS CLI is an important interface which can provide you with an easy mechanism for managing your AWS services. Your work is just to download and install this tool, and you will be in a position to control your numerous services which are running on the AWS. If you need to use the AWS CLI, it is a requirement that you first sign up for an AWS account. However, if you already have an account with AWS, then you don't have to create a new one, but you can go ahead to use the old account. It is after this that you can go ahead to install the AWS CLI.

You are provided with a number of ways to install the AWS CLI. This is determined by the kind of operating system which you are using. Note that the AWS CLI works by making API calls to the HTTPS (Hyper Text Transfer Protocol Secure), which is the secure version of HTTP. For such calls to be accomplished, you have to enable TCP port number 443 so as to allow for any outbound connections. It is good for you to ensure that you have done this before beginning to use the AWS CLI. Note that once you have created an account with the AWS, you should receive a message which will ask you to confirm whether the email is right. Of course, you will be making requests on the AWS, and these will be created programmatically. These have to be signed, and the Access keys, which are made up of a secret access key and the Access key Id are used for this purpose. You should ensure that these Access keys have been generated by the use of the AWS Management Console. You can then use them for the purpose of assigning the requests, and they will be allowed.

Made in the USA
Middletown, DE
09 August 2022

70950661R00046